The Moon's Gift

Victoria de Aboitiz

de Aboitiz, María Victoria

   The Moon's Gift - 1ªed. - Las Chacras : el autor, 2014.

   58 p. : il. ; 14 x 20 cm.

   ISBN 978-987-33-7802-7

   1. Literatura . I. Título

   CDD 860

Cataloging date: 22/01/2014

Cover: Afra

Editing and final design: Melisa Wortman on behalf of Chanchajistán <melisa@chanchajistan.com.ar>

Translator: Florencia Fernández Sanjurjo <ffsanjurjo@hotmail.com>

Cee FOREWORD ♥

When the seed of this book was planted, I never would have thought that some time later the English version would sprout from it and travel the world to meet girls of various lands and cultures.

The Moon's Gift began when many women asked if there was an English version available of the original work *Las Lunas*.

I am so grateful for your interest and support and especially for the embrace of sisterhood that transcends all limits.

I would like to acknowledge and thank my father Cosme and my sister Vero for their support and help with the book.

A very special thank you to Meli Wortman, the best editor ever.

May this book be a map that leads us to our female blessing.

Thank you,

VICTORIA
Argentina, 2016

❤ CONTENTS ᕮᕮ

Welcome

Puberty and adolescence are processes
of deep transformation. It happens to all of us,
and we all live it differently.

This little book intends to give you information
about the force that starts to flow within you.

It might be helpful to share this information with an
adult that accompanies and guides you.

I hope it's useful!

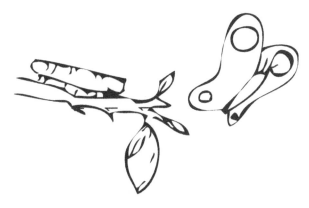

From Girl
to Woman

TRANSFORMATIONS

During puberty,
we are deeply transformed.

**From being Girls,
we become Women.**

...Hair starts to appear in our armpits and pubis.
Our nipples stiffen, our breasts grow and they
often hurt. We grow taller, our bodies get
roundish. Sometimes, pimples grow on our face
and our voice changes...

We also start feeling differently with ourselves
and with others. What used to be fun before
may not be that fun now. What we didn't
understand before, now we do. What we didn't
care about at all, now we do, and a lot.

These are times of intense growth and change.
Challenges, fears, joy, confusion ...

This period is called **puberty and adolescence,**
and it lasts approximately from
9 to 18 years old.

During this period, we go from one world to
another; or rather, from one way of being and
seeing the world to another.

IT IS PERFECTLY NORMAL THAT EVERYTHING SEEMS AWKWARD IN THIS STAGE.

It happened to every woman
and it will happen to every girl.

In nature, caterpillars turn into butterflies, and
they stop crawling to start flying. The same
happens to us, because the same Cycle rules
every being and we are part of it.

What you are living is important and special;

you are receiving the gift and
responsibility of being a woman

Understanding what happens during
these changes and during your cycle will give
you strength and confidence.

WELCOME!

Pubis mons
Ovaries
Pubic hair
Cycle
Vulva
Outer lips
Uterus
Bladder
Reproduction
Urethra
Inner lips
Fallopian tube
Clitoral hood
Vagina
Glands
Hormones
Clitoris
Fertile
Feelings
Menstruation
Cell
Process

DISCOVERING
YOURSELF

A GAME OF EXPLORATION

With calm, love, respect, and a little mirror,
you can see and feel the different textures
and sensations in the vulva and vagina.

You can start by looking at the hair that grows in the pubic mound or Mound of Venus, around the anus and covering the outer lips.

These thick outer lips surround the inner lips, which are soft and wet. They vary in color from woman to woman – ranging from brown to pink.

They join at the upper part of your vulva around the clitoris and its hood, a sort of fold of skin. This usually is the point of greatest sensitivity and pleasure of the whole genital area.

When you open the inner lips, you can see the vagina.

Place your fingers softly inside and you'll feel the vaginal walls. During the cycle, walls vary in moisture. Secretions help keep the vagina clean.

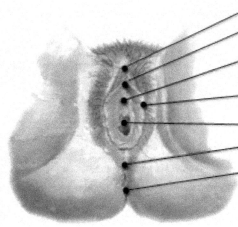

Clitoral hood
Clitoris
Urethral opening
Outer lips
Vaginal opening
Perineum
Anus

OUTER FEMALE SEXUAL ORGANS

INNER FEMALE SEXUAL ORGANS

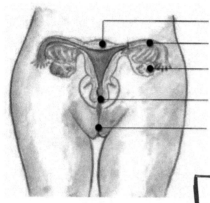

Uterus

Fallopian tube

Ovary

Cervix

Vagina

On each side of our uterus, we find the ovaries, which are connected by the Fallopian tubes.

Our ovaries are two glands that secret hormones and contain small bags called follicles. Inside each follicle there is an egg. The eggs are our most sacred cells, our creative seeds!

Every woman is born with approximately a million follicles that contain immature eggs inside.

The beginning of sexual development during puberty triggers the maturation of the first egg and, thus, the beginning of the first cycle, called *menarche.*

During this period, an egg matures each month, and the phenomenon repeats itself around 500 times throughout the whole reproductive life.

This condition marks the start of the fertile stage that extends to the last menstruations, called *menopause*.

Hormones are chemical substances that are released by our cells or glands. They are messengers that communicate through our body in order to trigger processes.

At the end of the vaginal canal, you find the cervix. The cervix is the base of the uterus. The cervix opening into the uterus is very small, but it is capable of expanding widely to give birth to a child.

If you lay a hand on your belly, you can feel your uterus. It is our wonderful muscular organ, approximately the size of a pear but capable of dilating to be home to a baby..

It is our second heart because it actually beats; it gives us strength and eagerness to create, to live. It is strong and flexible at the same time. It is our creative center of ideas, projects, and babies

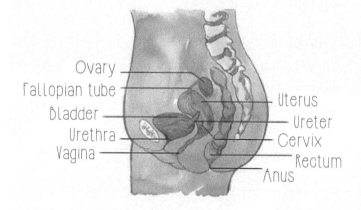

Ovary
Fallopian tube
Bladder
Urethra
Vagina

Uterus
Ureter
Cervix
Rectum
Anus

OUR GENITALS . . .

Our creative and sacred source.
Butterflies of life.
To enjoy, give, and receive pleasure,
with respect and self-love.

The Female Cycle

...THAT BRINGS BALANCE
AND RENEWAL...

Follicular Phase
OVULATION

THE GROWING MOON, LIKE A FLASHLIGHT IN THE DARK,
GUIDES THE NIGHTS AND OUR BODIES.
SPRING APPEARS IN THE NEW GREEN OF THE PLANTS, IN THE
FLIGHT OF BUTTERFLIES, AND THE CREATIVITY OF WOMEN.

Around 10 to 20 follicles with eggs inside start maturing. Usually, only one develops completely. The follicle starts secreting **estrogen** and **progesterone** hormones and moves towards the ovary's surface.

FULL MOON IN THE SKY, SUMMER ON THE SKIN AND THE
RICHNESS OF THE FRUITS HANG FROM THE TREES.
THE EARTH IS FERTILE AND READY TO CREATE. WOMEN, TOO.

The follicle and the ovarian surface open for the ovulation to occur. Sometimes, when it occurs, we can feel a light stitch-like pain in the ovary! The released egg travels a few days through one of the tubes towards the uterus.

WE ARE FERTILE only in this short period of the cycle. The secreted hormones stimulate the growth of the uterus' endometrium due to the increased blood flow and the production of nourishing substances by glands, in case the egg is fertilized.

Luteal Phase
MENSTRUATION

THE WANING MOON CROSSES THE SKY DURING AUTUMN WINDS.
LEAVES CHANGE COLOR AND TEXTURE AND NECESSARILY FALL
TO NOURISH THE EARTH, WHERE THE ROOTS GROW.

If the egg is not inseminated, it will also fall to fertilize our earth and nourish our roots. The remains of the follicle left behind (also called **corpeus luteum** or **yellow body**) will produce hormones for a few more days. When production starts declining, the small arteries and veins of the linen of the uterus open because they don't receive any more nutrients. Menstruation is about to come. Women retreat to their inner selves. They know that menstruation is close and their feelings and emotions heighten.

THE NEW MOON CANNOT BE SEEN IN THE DARKNESS OF WINTER
NIGHTS. EVERYTHING IS QUIET AND DEEP. THE PLANT'S SAP HAS GONE
TO THE EARTH'S DEPTHS TO REST AND THE ANIMALS HIBERNATE;
THERE'S ONLY SILENCE

WOMEN QUIET DOWN. MENSTRUATION ARRIVES. IT IS TIME TO LET GO.
THE EARTH, THE MOON, AND WOMEN ARE RESTING
AND RENEWING THEMSELVES.

WELCOME TO THE GREAT CYCLE THAT RULES

DAY 1

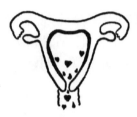

MENSTRUATION

NEW MOON

WINTER

DAYS 7, 8, 9...

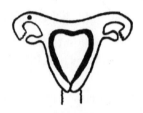

THE EGG MATURES.
THE ENDOMETRIUM
THICKENS.

WAXING MOON

SPRING

THE UNIVERSE, THE MOON, THE EARTH AND WOMEN

DAYS 13, 14, 15...

DAYS 27, 28, 29...

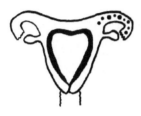

OVULATION

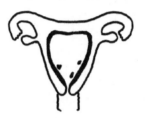

THE EGG DISSOLVES
AND THE LINING IS
RELEASED.

FULL MOON

WANING MOON

SUMMER

AUTUMN

(You are part of the whole)

* People around the world see the Moon in different ways!

In the previous pages, the Moon is represented as seen from the Southern hemisphere.

If you are in the Northern hemisphere, you'll see her like this:

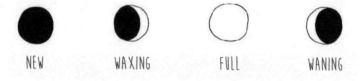

NEW   WAXING   FULL   WANING

Welcoming Menstruation

WHAT ARE THE DREAMS YOU WANT
TO CREATE WHEN YOU
BECOME A WOMAN?

The first menstruation is a very special Initiation passage, which may trigger different emotions: joy, pride, fear, denial, indifference, or a combination of all of them! Beyond these different emotions, something wonderful is taking place.

THE FORCE OF THE CYCLE IS STARTING TO FLOW THROUGH YOU!

You are growing well and you are healthy.
You are a girl on the path to becoming a woman.
Let yourself be driven by the force that
lives inside you; there's nothing you
must specifically do or be.
It happens by itself.

With patience, cycle to cycle,
we learn to be Women.

We transform ourselves
more and more into beaming
and creative women!

MENSTRUATION IN DIFFERENT CULTURES

BY SOPHIA STYLE

IMAGINE THAT YOU ARE AN APACHE GIRL ♥ ℓℓ૭

The day you start menstruating, you feel proud because you know that the whole village will celebrate it with you. You go to your godmother's cabin with an eagle feather to give her the news. She will teach you everything you need to know to become a woman. First, you go to a special cabin and you stay there alone for a while.

You do a fast to clean your body. When you are ready, your godmother explains to you that you are menstruating because you are now fertile and you can have your own children.

She teaches you many things about menstruation, fertility, sexuality, contraception, and female rituals. While you are learning from her, women prepare a special gown for you. Your godmother gets you ready for the ceremony, teaching you a special dance. Last, there is a big celebration with all the community. You receive plenty of gifts and blessings, and later, as a "life-giver", you give your blessing to the tribe.

NOW, LET US GO TO A TO THE AIARY TRIBE, IN BRAZIL ♥ ℓℓ૭

When you announce the arrival of your first period, all your family and friends gather with you. Your mother symbolically cuts your braids and everybody asks you for hair for good luck. During a month, until your next menstruation, you can only eat bread and fish, to purify your body and mind. Upon your second menstruation, your father gets up at dawn and sings a special song, inviting the whole village to a party where you can eat everything you want!

Source: www.mujerciclica.com

WE CONTINUE OUR TRIP, CROSSING THE ATLANTIC OCEAN

We arrive to Nigeria, with the Tiv tribe. The day of your first cycle, the community sees you as giver of fertility and bearer of good luck. You walk over all the fields in the village, blessing the soil and fostering a good harvest.

During a ceremony in your honor, you receive a fertility tattoo under your belly button. From that moment on, you show it proudly to the world, demonstrating that you are no longer a girl.

NOW, WE CROSS THE INDIAN OCEAN AND WE END OUR JOURNEY IN SRI LANKA

Here, you take a special bath the day of your first menstruation. Thus, you are no longer a girl and you come out of the bath as a young woman. You wear a white dress, the color of your initiation. Your family prepares a celebration, where you receive many gifts and wishes for a happy, healthy and prosperous life.

ALL THESE GIRLS CELEBRATE THE COMING OF MENARCHE IN DIFFERENT WAYS, WITH THEIR FAMILIES AND COMMUNITY. HOW WOULD YOU LIKE TO CELEBRATE YOUR MENARCHE? WITH WHO? IS THERE A SPECIAL PLACE YOU WOULD LIKE TO GO TO?

IDEAS TO CELEBRATE MENARCHE
FOR GIRLS, MOMS, AUNTS, FRIENDS, DADS, AND SIBLINGS

It's really very personal how each one of you will feel when your period arrives and how you'll want to share the news. It's likely that some of you will share the news with just a few people and live it in a silent way. Others will be very excited and willing to tell everyone!

Without a doubt, although you may feel a full range of mixed emotions regarding your period, it will be a very special occasion that you'll remember throughout your life. Your family and friends will be deeply and personally moved as well, and they'll express their feelings according to their personality.

Those of you who already had your **menarche** ⟶ FIRST MENSTRUATION

How did you feel? What happened?

- - - - - - - - - - - -

Below, there are some ideas to recognize, commemorate, or celebrate your coming of age. Please feel free to modify and adapt them to who you are!

- ✸ Outing to a special place with friends and/or family.
- ✸ Make a trip, it could be a women's journey!
- ✸ Make her a gift, an amulet to commemorate the occasion.
- ✸ Express your love and feelings.
- ✸ Write her a letter. You could include anecdotes of your female lineage, your own menarche, drawings, pictures, etc. Fathers can write about their feelings regarding womanhood.
- ✸ Gift her a "red" notebook with her menarche's date for her to write and draw about her transformation.
- ✸ Gather with friends and loved adults to celebrate and talk.

WHAT IDEAS DO YOU HAVE?

HOW TO ACCOMPANY AND DISCUSS OUR KIDS'
SEXUALITY

* Be clear and simple *
* Be available *
* Call things by their names *
* Speak with the truth *

Our personal history and paradigm affect our sexuality and how we manage to accompany our kids.

As adults, it's important to know ourselves with sincerity and if we wish, work on our history to walk along as awake as possible!

It's very important to respect and perceive how each kid lives his/her journey, and avoid projecting onto them what we would have liked to experience.

We can try to avoid forcing situations and emotions, and work with what is real, with who we are, how we relate and with what we truly feel.

MENSTRUATION,
◄◄◄◄◄◄◄◄◄◄◄ WISE BALANCING FORCE

IN ORDER TO THRIVE, SUMMER NEEDS WINTER.
AND THE LEAVES THAT FALL IN AUTUMN WILL
FERTILIZE THE PLANTS THAT GROW IN SPRING.

With menstruation, we let go of not only tissue and blood but everything we don't need anymore from our emotions and energies. This sometimes happens unnoticed and other times we are aware of it.

A woman's cycle varies from 24 to 35 days. We count day 1 as the first day of the period. Generally, we ovulate around day 14 and we menstruate again around day 28 (see pages 28/29), although there are variations from month to month.

Menstruation itself may last between 2 to 7 days. Months or years may pass from the menarche until the cycle regularizes.

On the other hand, our cycle may alter if something emotionally intense happens to us. For instance, menstruation may take place in advance or after it should happen. The cycle is our reflection; it is a great self-discovery tool.

Each one of us experiences menstruation in a unique way, and each time it may happen in a different manner. Sometimes we don't even notice it's about to take place and it surprises us; other times, we feel discomfort a few days in advance.

FEELINGS ▷▷▷▷▷▷▷▷▷▷

There may be some patterns that repeat themselves as well. For example, the days before menstruating: more eagerness to eat, sensations in the uterus and waist, emotional and bodily sensitivity, spiritual clarity, etc. Near ovulation time: more energetic, more impulses, and sexual pleasure.

Each one of you will recognize specific sensations and will respond to them, communicating with yourselves.

EMOTIONS

The days before you menstruate, emotions and sensations usually intensify. This may happen because when we menstruate we connect more deeply with our body, and our body is part of our emotional processes. It is a perfect moment to observe and let go.

Throughout your many cycles, you will notice that this tool for self-discovery and renovation is very healing because it keeps us balanced. It makes us release everything we no longer need.

LOVE OFFERING

MYSTERIES

Through our cycle, we can discover ourselves and be more in contact with our inner world. This inner space is where our ideas and eagerness to create are born. There, secrets are whispered and we start revealing and discovering our gifts and our purposes. Dreams may be clear messengers, so listen and trust them!

IF YOU FEEL DISCOMFORT OR PAIN WHEN YOU ARE ABOUT TO MENSTRUATE, YOU CAN:

* Lay face down on the ground
* Put a hot water bottle on your uterus and/or the lower part of your back
* Rest, do nothing
* Enjoy rest
* Eat healthy. Avoid refined foods: sugar and white flour
* Avoid junk food: sodas, candies, fried food
* Breathe and take the air to the uterus
* Draw and write what you are feeling
* Sing

WHAT DOES YOUR BODY ASK FOR? WHAT ABOUT YOUR EMOTIONS?

Natural Alternatives

PLANTS

PLANTS ARE GENEROUS AND WISE BEINGS.
THEY CAN BE GOOD FRIENDS THAT WILL
HELP YOU IF YOU LET THEM.

Drink **cinnamon, chamomile,
rosemary** or **marigold** infusion,
You can research the
native plants in your area
or consult with a naturopath
for deeper guidance.

HOW TO PREPARE
AN INFUSION:

Put half a spoonful of dry leaves
(if the leaves are fresh, use more)
per cup of water at boiling point.
Cover the cup for 2 minutes to
prevent the evaporation of the oils,
filter and drink.

Artemisia is a special aromatic
plant for women. It is a great
female hormones regulator
and, if you ask her, she will
help with your female processes.

ECOLOGICAL PADS

ECOLOGICAL PRODUCTS FOR MENSTRUATION

Throughout time, women have used different forms of menstrual protection. Until the surge of disposable pads, every woman used a sort of reusable sanitary towel.

Nowadays, disposable pads are practical, comfortable and easy. Sometimes I use them. But many disposable sanitary towels and tampons include toxic substances in their preparation and in their components that contaminate water and soil.

We also know that plastic may take up to 500 years to degrade! What harms the Earth inevitably affects us.

In addition, these pads alienate us from our body because we don't get in touch with our menstrual fluid when we use them. We directly throw our blood to the garbage.

ECOLOGICAL ALTERNATIVES FOR THE BLEEDING DAYS ARE REUSABLE PADS MADE OF CLOTH AND THE MENSTRUAL CUP.

Instead of "throwing away" your blood to the garbage, you can give it to the earth: water a flowerbed or a vegetable garden. Your blood is full of nutrients and it will nourish the earth instead of contaminating it. **This connects you with the earth, and may be your offering to her.**

There's also the reusable menstrual cup, which goes inside the vagina. It is made of hypoallergenic silicone and it's safe for internal use. This cup collects the blood, it doesn't absorb it. Depending on the quantity of fluid, you empty it 2 or 4 times a day.

HOW TO MAKE YOUR OWN CLOTH PADS

There are different types of eco-pads.
Here are two models.

HOLDER

1. With an old piece of cloth, draw the template of the holder. The approximate measurements are 20 cm long and 15 cm wide, leaving a few centimeters for sewing. Cut two templates (to be more resistant) and sew them on the edges.

2. On the wings, sew snaps or a piece of Velcro to hold it onto your underwear.

3. To hold the towel to the pad, you can sew two elastic strips (very tight) or Velcro on each end of the pad.

ABSORBENT

1. With a towel, a piece of cotton cloth, or any kind of soft and absorbent cloth, cut a rectangle. The size varies according to what each woman prefers —approximately 15-20 cm long and 4 cm wide—.

2. Like the pad, cut 2 or 3 layers and sew them on the edges. The more layers, the more absorbent. Ready!

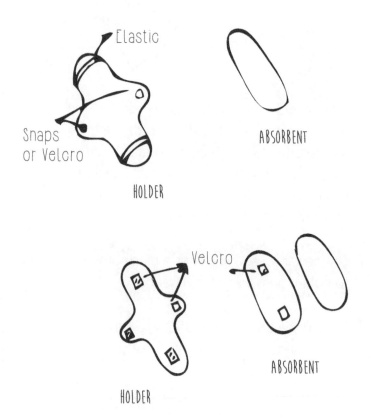

Elastic

Snaps
or Velcro

HOLDER

ABSORBENT

Velcro

HOLDER

ABSORBENT

CLEANING

Leave the pads to soak in a recipient with water a few hours. For deeper cleaning, add lemon drops or salt to the water. If the stain won't leave, put hydrogen peroxide directly on it for a few minutes. Then, hand-wash it and hang it to dry, best under the sun.

Many women use cloth pads and each one washes them in a different way.

DISCOVER THE BEST WAY FOR YOU!

In these web sites you will find more instructions about making your own pads:

> http://tipnut.com/free-pattern-for-washable-feminine-menstrual-pads/
> https://sites.google.com/site/shewhorunsinthef orest/006

SACRED BLOOD

Menstrual blood contains the cells of your body —in other words, the seeds of your Being—.

Menstrual blood is Sacred. Your blood means that you are a giver of life, fertile and a creator.

In addition, it is full of nutrients that are rich for the Earth and plants. Offer your blood to the Earth and you'll feel connected to her.

Watch your Cycle

On this chart, you will be able to SEE the rhythm of your cycle by marking the days of bleeding.
The intelligence and wisdom of our body keeps amazing me! Also the fact that we respond
to the cycles of the moon and nature. Our bodies are not the only ones responding to cycles, our
relationships and projects are, too!

Month	1	2	3	4	5	6	7	8	9	10	11	12	13	14	15	16	17	18	19	20	21	22	23	24	25	26	27	28	29	30	31
JANUARY	1	2	3	4	5	6	7	8	9	10	11	12	13	14	15	16	17	18	19	20	21	22	23	24	25	26	27	28	29	30	31
FEBRUARY	1	2	3	4	5	6	7	8	9	10	11	12	13	14	15	16	17	18	19	20	21	22	23	24	25	26	27	28	29		
MARCH	1	2	3	4	5	6	7	8	9	10	11	12	13	14	15	16	17	18	19	20	21	22	23	24	25	26	27	28	29	30	31
APRIL	1	2	3	4	5	6	7	8	9	10	11	12	13	14	15	16	17	18	19	20	21	22	23	24	25	26	27	28	29	30	
MAY	1	2	3	4	5	6	7	8	9	10	11	12	13	14	15	16	17	18	19	20	21	22	23	24	25	26	27	28	29	30	31
JUNE	1	2	3	4	5	6	7	8	9	10	11	12	13	14	15	16	17	18	19	20	21	22	23	24	25	26	27	28	29	30	
JULY	1	2	3	4	5	6	7	8	9	10	11	12	13	14	15	16	17	18	19	20	21	22	23	24	25	26	27	28	29	30	31
AUGUST	1	2	3	4	5	6	7	8	9	10	11	12	13	14	15	16	17	18	19	20	21	22	23	24	25	26	27	28	29	30	31
SEPTEMBER	1	2	3	4	5	6	7	8	9	10	11	12	13	14	15	16	17	18	19	20	21	22	23	24	25	26	27	28	29	30	
OCTOBER	1	2	3	4	5	6	7	8	9	10	11	12	13	14	15	16	17	18	19	20	21	22	23	24	25	26	27	28	29	30	31
NOVEMBER	1	2	3	4	5	6	7	8	9	10	11	12	13	14	15	16	17	18	19	20	21	22	23	24	25	26	27	28	29	30	
DECEMBER	1	2	3	4	5	6	7	8	9	10	11	12	13	14	15	16	17	18	19	20	21	22	23	24	25	26	27	28	29	30	31

CYCLES REPEAT THEMSELVES ETERNALLY ...

Throughout our cycles, as moons pass by, we keep learning to listen to ourselves and to be synchronized with Earth's cycles.

Understanding cycles and flowing with them gives us Peace and Wellbeing.

May you enjoy
the Magic that
flows through you!

BIBLIOGRAPHY

Northrup, Christiane. *Cuerpo de Mujer, Sabiduría de Mujer*, Urano, 2010.

Pérez San Martín, Pabla. *Manual Introductorio a la Ginecología Natural*, Ginecosofía, 2015.

Owen, Lara. *Honoring Menstruation*, The Crossing Press, 1998.

Colectivo de Mujeres de Boston.
Nuestros cuerpos, nuestras vidas.
Anatomía y fisiología de la sexualidad y la reproducción, The Collective, 1981.